NORWAY

By Jagger Youssef
and Carol Hand

EXPLORING WORLD CULTURES

Cavendish Square

Published in 2027 by Cavendish Square Publishing, LLC
2544 Clinton Street, Buffalo, NY 14224

Second Edition

Website: cavendishsq.com

Library of Congress Cataloging-in-Publication Data

Names: Youssef, Jagger author | Hand, Carol, 1945- author
Title: Norway / Jagger Youssef and Carol Hand.
Description: New York : Cavendish Square Publishing, [2027] | Series: Exploring world cultures | Includes index.
Identifiers: LCCN 2026005196 (print) | LCCN 2026005197 (ebook) | ISBN 9781502677112 library binding | ISBN 9781502677105 paperback | ISBN 9781502677129 ebook
Subjects: LCSH: Norway--Civilization
Classification: LCC DL409 .Y68 2027 (print) | LCC DL409 (ebook) | DDC 948.1--dc23/eng/20260312
LC record available at https://lccn.loc.gov/2026005196
LC ebook record available at https://lccn.loc.gov/2026005197

Writers: Jagger Youssef; Carol Hand (second edition)
Editor: Therese Shea
Designer: Deanna Lepovich

The photographs in this book are used by permission and through the courtesy of: Cover Tomsickova Tatyana/Shutterstock.com; p. 4 Denis Belitsky/Shutterstock.com; p. 5 Andrei Armiagov/Shutterstock.com; p. 6 Dear Lady-Deer/Shutterstock.com; p. 7 fokke baarssen/Shutterstock.com; p. 8 Miscellany on the Life of St. Edmund- MS M.736 fol. 9v/Wikimedia Commons; p. 9 piemags/ww2archive/Alamy Photos; p. 10 Anne-Marie Forker/Alamy Photos; p. 11 Damien VERRIER/Shutterstock.com; p. 12 Krakenimages.com/Shutterstock.com; p. 13 Saskia B/Shutterstock.com; p. 14 Travel Faery/Shutterstock.com; p. 15 Xseon/Shutterstock.com; p. 16 Tina Manley/Alamy Photos; p. 17 Tomasz Podolski/Shutterstock.com; p. 18 Popova Valeriya/Shutterstock.com; p. 19 makasana photo/Shutterstock.com; p. 20 Mariusz Switulski/Alamy Photos; p. 21 F1online digitale Bildagentur GmbH/Alamy Photos; p. 22 Anders Ryman/Alamy Photos; p. 23 Tomasz Majchrowicz/Shutterstock.com; p. 24 fotografcic/Shutterstock.com; p. 25 dibrova/Shutterstock.com; p. 27 (top) Orange Pictures/Shutterstock.com; p. 27 (bottom) Anne-Marie Forker/Alamy Photos; p. 28 knelson20/Shutterstock.com; p. 29 Aleksandra Suzi/Shutterstock.com.

CPSIA compliance information: Batch #CS27CSQ: For further information contact Cavendish Square Publishing LLC at 1-877-980-4450.

Printed in United States of America

CONTENTS

Introduction 4
Chapter 1 Geography 6
Chapter 2 History 8
Chapter 3 Government 10
Chapter 4 The Economy 12
Chapter 5 The Environment 14
Chapter 6 The People Today 16
Chapter 7 Lifestyle 18
Chapter 8 Religion 20
Chapter 9 Language 22
Chapter 10 Arts and Festivals 24
Chapter 11 Fun and Play 26
Chapter 12 Food 28
Glossary 30
Find Out More 31
Index 32

INTRODUCTION

Norway is a country in northern Europe with a long history. It was home to the Vikings. These were the **raiders**, explorers, and traders who were feared by other Europeans. The country is still connected to its past through its royal family, headed by a king.

Norway is known for its great beauty, including snowy mountains, icy glaciers, and steep valleys. People try to spend as much time in nature as possible. Still, most people live in cities.

Another name for the northern lights is the aurora borealis. It can be seen from September to March in northern Norway.

During the winter, the people of Norway can see the northern lights in parts of the country closer to the Arctic. They can also see the "midnight sun." That's when the sun doesn't set in summer. And some winter days have no sunrise!

Norway's **economy** is strong. Most people have a job and live well. This nation is among the happiest in the world. Read on to learn more about this interesting place.

Norway's beauty draws millions of tourists, or visitors from other countries.

GEOGRAPHY

Norway shares borders with Sweden, Finland, and Russia. Norway and Sweden make up the Scandinavian **Peninsula**. The Barents Sea, North Sea, Norwegian Sea, and Baltic Sea surround the peninsula.

An ocean current keeps Norway much warmer than other northern parts of the world. Still, Norway gets lots of snow in the winter. Steep mountains run down Norway's center. The tallest is Galdhøpiggen at 8,100 feet (2,469 meters). Norway has lots of forests and valleys too.

FACT!

About 80 percent of Norway is above 1,500 feet (460 m). It's very mountainous.

The coast of Norway has around 50,000 islands.

Northern Norway is **tundra**. It's too cold for trees to grow there. The soil stays frozen all year long. In the south, the land is flatter and better for farming.

Norway has many lakes. The largest is called Lake Mjøsa. Norway also has rivers. The longest is the Glomma River. Norway is best known for its many fjords. These are long, deep, narrow bodies of water that reach far inland.

Glaciers carved fjords over millions of years. Norway has more than 1,000 fjords.

INTERESTING ANIMALS

Reindeer, wolverines, and seabirds live in Norway. Polar bears live on Norway's Svalbard Islands, in the far north.

HISTORY

People have lived in Norway for more than 8,000 years. They fished, hunted, and later farmed. During the late eighth and ninth centuries CE, Vikings from Norway invaded England, Scotland, Ireland, and France. They built towns there. Vikings were warriors, traders, and explorers. They were excellent ship builders too.

FACT!
The Viking Age lasted from about 800 to 1050 CE.

Kings ruled Norway for hundreds of years. For some of this time, Norway was part of Sweden, Denmark, or both. Norway became its own country in 1905, and Haakon VII was crowned Norway's king.

This art of Vikings on the water dates back to the 1100s.

Germany controlled Norway during World War II (1939–1945). In 1969, oil was discovered in Norway's part of the North Sea. As more oil and gas fields were found, Norway's economy boomed.

German troops keep watch in the mountains of Norway during World War II.

KING OLAF

Olaf II Haraldsson was king of Norway around 1000 CE. He helped bring the nation together under one ruler. He also spread Christianity, or the belief in Jesus Christ.

GOVERNMENT

Norway's government is called a constitutional monarchy. That means the government has a constitution, or national set of governing laws, and a monarch, or king or queen. In fact, Norway's official name is the Kingdom of Norway.

Norway's government has three branches. The executive branch runs the government. It's led by a prime minister. The country's king or queen is also part of the executive branch.

Harald V has been king of Norway since 1991. His son Prince Haakon will take the role next.

The capital of Norway is the city of Oslo.

FACT!

Norway's constitution was passed in 1814. It has been amended, or changed, over the years.

The legislative branch is made up of a parliament, or law-making body, called the Storting. These men and women serve for four years at a time.

The judicial branch is made up of courts. The courts explain the laws. The highest court is the Supreme Court. The country's 19 counties have local governments.

THE MONARCH'S JOB

Norway's monarch doesn't work in the government. The monarch takes part in events as a symbol of the country.

THE ECONOMY

Norway's economy has many key parts. The largest are oil and gas. Fishing and **hydroelectric** power are also important.

Oil has made Norway one of the world's richest countries. Some money from the sale of oil is used to help Norway's people, called Norwegians. About 10 percent of workers in Norway have jobs in the oil industry—the group of businesses and other services that deal with oil.

FACT!

About 200,000 Norwegians have jobs connected to the nation's oil industry.

Norwegian currency, or money, is called the krone. More than one is called kroner.

The biggest industry in Norway is the services industry. Over 78 percent of workers are in a service job. These include tour guides, hotel workers, teachers, doctors, and others who help people.

Norway also has lots of seafood. Norwegians eat a lot of fish. They **export** it too. In fact, Norway is the world's second-largest exporter of seafood, behind China.

Tourism, the business of bringing in visitors, is another important part of Norway's economy.

TRADE PARTNERS

Norway trades the most with these nations: Germany, the United Kingdom, Sweden, Denmark, China, the Netherlands, and the United States.

THE ENVIRONMENT

About one-fourth of Norway is covered with forests. Fewer trees are found in the mountains and in the north. With its forests, fjords, mountains, and rivers, nature in Norway is beautiful. But the country also has **environmental** problems.

Norway is a big producer of oil and gas. Burning them puts harmful gases, such as carbon dioxide and methane, into the air. These gases hurt the environment and raise Earth's temperature.

Rising sea levels are another environmental problem that Norway must deal with.

Most of Norway's electricity comes from hydroelectric energy, or power. This is much cleaner than using gas or oil, but it can still cause problems, such as water pollution and harm to nature.

Norwegians are trying to do more to help the environment. For example, they're passing laws to protect coasts from oil spills. More wind farms and other kinds of **renewable** energy are being used too.

FACT!

Nearly all of Norway's electricity comes from the renewable resources of water and wind.

Norway is trying to protect rivers by limiting where dams can be built.

NORWAY'S NEW CARS

In 2025, 96 percent of new cars sold in Norway were electric vehicles (EVs). These pollute less than gas-powered cars.

THE PEOPLE TODAY

Norway is home to about 5.5 million people. That's not a lot compared to many other countries. About 82 percent of Norway's people are **ethnic** Norwegians. That means their family line can be traced back to the Vikings.

The Sámi live in northern parts of Norway, Finland, and Sweden.

THE SÁMI CULTURE

About 60,000 people in Norway are Native People called Sámi. They've lived in northern Norway for thousands of years. They have their own language and culture, or way of life.

In the 21st century, people from other parts of the world are moving to Norway. Most are from Eastern Europe or the Middle East.

More than 85 percent of people in Norway live in cities. The largest city is its capital, Oslo. Just over 1 million people live there. It has airports, tall buildings, and businesses, and the parliament meets there. Living in Oslo is very costly.

FACT!

The second-largest city is Bergen, on the west coast of the country.

This is a view of Oslo, with the Royal Palace in the background.

LIFESTYLE

Norway is often one of the top countries in the World Happiness Report. Norwegians work, have fun, and enjoy time relaxing.

All children must go to school for at least ten years. It starts when they are five or six years old. There are three stages of school: primary, lower secondary, and upper secondary. Students often go to college after secondary school. There are many excellent universities in Norway.

Norwegians enjoy gathering at home or out in their community.

Norway's great beauty is a reason given for people's happiness living there.

FACT!

In Norway, the word *friluftsliv* (outdoor life) means life is best lived outside in nature.

Norway has long worked hard to make sure men and women are treated the same, or equally. Laws protect people's rights.

The word *kos* sums up life for Norwegians. It has many meanings, but mostly means "happy togetherness." Norwegians enjoy their community and don't worry too much about the future.

GETTING AROUND

Norwegians travel by bus, train, and ferry. One train company in Norway takes people to the Arctic Circle. Some Norwegians travel by boat to cities or countries nearby.

RELIGION

Most Norwegians are Christians. The country's first constitution required citizens to follow the Lutheran branch of Christianity. Other religions weren't allowed. In 1964, the constitution was amended to say anyone could believe in any religion or in no religion at all.

FACT!

The early Norwegians practiced the Norse religion, which had many gods including Thor.

Heddal Stave Church was founded about 1200. It's the largest of the stave churches.

About 67 percent of Norwegians belong to the Church of Norway, also called Evangelical Lutheran. About 3 percent are Roman Catholic, and another 3 percent are Muslim. Even smaller percentages follow other religions, including Judaism, Buddhism, and Hinduism. About 10 percent of Norwegians don't follow a religion.

Christian churches are found all over Norway. Some are very old. Special wooden churches, called stave churches, combine Viking and Christian styles. About twenty-eight stave churches remain today.

NEW CULTURES, NEW RELIGIONS

Immigrants coming into the country have brought their religions, including Buddhism and Islam.

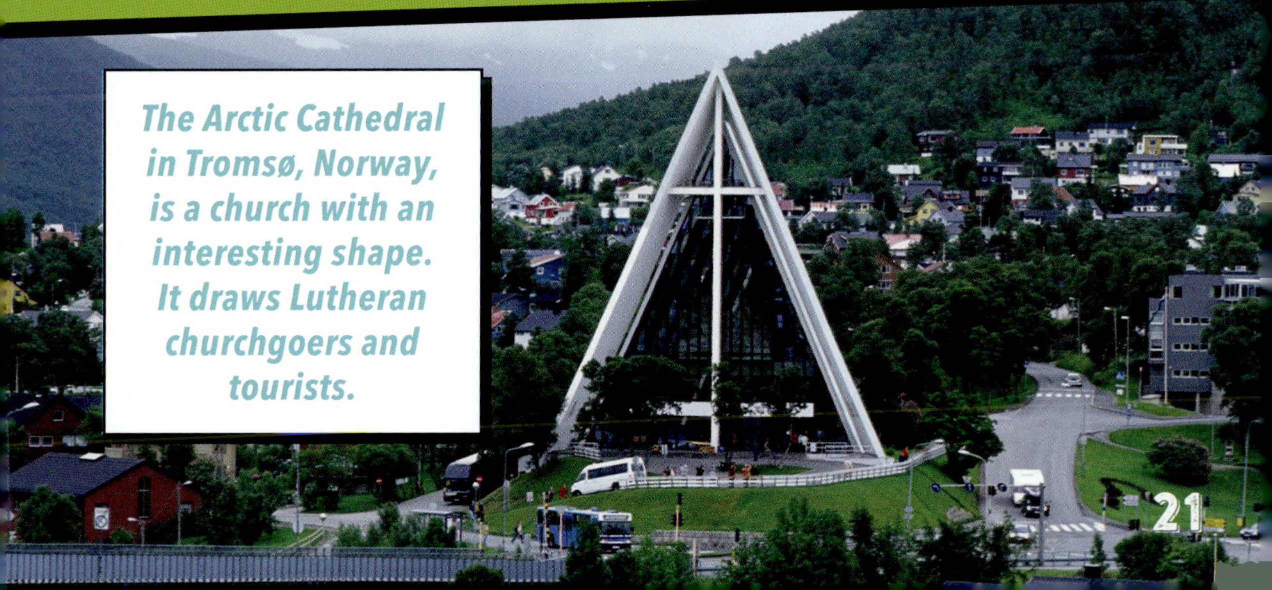

The Arctic Cathedral in Tromsø, Norway, is a church with an interesting shape. It draws Lutheran churchgoers and tourists.

LANGUAGE

The Norwegian and Sámi people have two different languages. Both are official languages of the country. Most people in Norway speak Norwegian. It sounds and looks like Swedish or Danish. The language of Sámi is spoken in northern and central Norway by the Sámi.

There are three types, or dialects, of Sámi spoken in Norway. Here, a boy learns the Sámi written language.

SPEAKING SÁMI

People who speak Sámi also speak Norwegian. Sámi is very different from Norwegian, though.

There are two ways to write Norwegian. Bokmål is based on written Danish. Most people use this form of Norwegian. Nynorsk was created in the 1850s. It's used most often on the west coast of Norway. People who understand Bokmål can understand Nynorsk.

People who move to Norway from other countries speak their home languages. In addition, many Norwegians learn other languages. These include English, German, and French. English is the second most widely spoken language.

FACT!

People who speak Norwegian, Danish, or Swedish can understand one another because the languages are so alike.

The Norwegian alphabet has three letters not in the English alphabet: Æ, Ø, and Å.

ARTS AND FESTIVALS

Norway's holidays celebrate many events and beliefs. Religious holidays include Christmas and Easter. New Year's Eve is full of fireworks and family gatherings. National holidays such as Labor Day on May 1 and Constitution Day on May 17 have parades.

Norway has many exciting music, arts, and culture festivals. Bergenfest is in Bergen in June each year. It features musicians from around the world. Musikkfest in Oslo in June features more than forty stages around the city.

Norwegians celebrating Constitution Day may wear special cultural clothing.

FACT!

The Midgardsblot festival in August near Oslo celebrates Viking culture and heavy metal music.

Bergen's Festival of Lights (Lysfesten) marks the beginning of the Christmas season.

The country also has classical music, ballet, and theater productions. The Tromsø International Film Festival shows movies from around the world. Tromsø's Northern Lights Festival combines folk music with views of the northern lights. Food festivals are also popular, including the Trøndelag Food Festival in Trondheim.

WINTER FUN

Winter is cold in Norway. Some festivals celebrate this. In February, musicians in Lillehammer perform with **instruments** of ice!

FUN AND PLAY

Norwegians like to spend much of their free time outdoors. Cross-country skiing is the most popular sport. Soccer and **handball** are top sports too. Boating and other kinds of skiing are also activities enjoyed in this country. In addition, Norwegians run, cycle, and swim.

Many Norwegians own a cabin. They go there to take hikes and long walks. However, they also like to relax. They enjoy quiet activities such as reading and playing board games.

Norwegians love to go to concerts. Bands such as A-ha, Aqua, and Röyksopp found success worldwide. Popular singers in Norway today include Aurora and Astrid S.

OLYMPIC SUCCESS

Norway has won over 500 Olympic medals. It has won more Winter Olympics medals than other country.

More than half of Norway's Winter Olympics medals have come from cross-country skiing and speed skating.

FACT!

In Norway, many adults have 25 or more vacation days every year. They often go on summer trips to other countries.

Soccer is popular in Norway. Erling Haaland is a Norwegian pro who plays for Manchester City and the Norway national team.

FOOD

Norwegian foods are linked to Norway's natural world. For example, Norway's coast and bodies of water make fish easy to get. Herring—a kind of fish—is often **pickled** and served in sauces. Cod is another fish Norwegians eat in different ways, including rolled into balls called *fiskeboller*. The national dish of Norway is *fårikål*. It contains lamb, cabbage, and potatoes. Norwegians, especially the Sámi of the north, eat reindeer meat.

A **krumkake** *is a thin rolled cookie. It's sometimes stuffed with chocolate, cream, or jam.*

For sweet treats, Norwegians love wild berries, including strawberries, blackberries, and cloudberries, as well as homemade waffles. In modern times, food from other cultures can also be found. Fast-food restaurants are popular in many cities. However, Norwegian foods remain an important part of special events and holidays.

FACT!

Cloudberries are a kind of berry that grows in cold places and even near the Arctic.

Lutefisk is a cod dish often eaten at Christmas.

MADE BY VIKINGS

Some Norwegian foods can be linked to the Vikings. These include *lefse*, a flatbread, and *skyr*, a kind of cheese that looks like yogurt.

GLOSSARY

economy: The money made in an area and how it is made.

environmental: Dealing with the natural world around us.

ethnic: Relating to a group of people that have the same cultural background.

export: To send and sell goods to another country.

handball: A game in which a ball is hit with the hand in a walled court.

hydroelectric: Energy that is produced from moving water.

immigrant: One who comes to a country to settle there.

instrument: An object used to make music.

peninsula: A narrow piece of land that extends into water from the mainland.

pickle: To add a mixture of vinegar or salt to a food to make it last longer.

raider: One who suddenly attacks.

renewable: Having to do with sources of power like the sun or wind that can be used over and over again and won't run out.

tundra: An area with frozen soil and no trees.

FIND OUT MORE

Books

Gillespie, Katie. *Norway*. New York, NY: Lightbox Learning, 2024.

Van, R. L. *Norway*. Minneapolis, MN: Big Buddy Books, 2023.

Websites

Norway
kids.nationalgeographic.com/explore/countries/norway
National Geographic Kids provides information about Norway's geography, history, and other topics.

Norway
*www.kids-world-travel-guide.com/norway-facts.html*National
Check out easy-to-read facts and hear Norway's national anthem on this site.

Video

Norway: A Time-Lapse Adventure
thekidshouldseethis.com/post/norway-a-time-lapse-adventure
This video shows the landscapes of Norway.

INDEX

A

Arctic, 5, 19, 29

B

Bergen, 17, 24, 25
borders, 6

C

constitution, 10, 11, 20
Constitution Day, 24

F

fjords, 7, 14

G

gas, 9, 12, 14, 15
glaciers, 4, 7

H

Haakon VII, King, 8
Haaland, Erling, 27
happiness, 5, 18, 19
Harald V, King, 10

K

kings, 4, 8, 9, 10

M

mountains, 4, 6, 9, 14
music, 24, 25

N

northern lights, 4, 5, 25

O

oil, 9, 12, 14, 15
Olaf II Haraldsson, 9
Olympics, 26, 27
Oslo, 11, 17, 24, 25

P

parliament, 11, 17
pollution, 15

S

Sámi, 16, 22, 28
soccer, 26, 27

V

Vikings, 4, 8, 16, 21, 25, 29